© 1990 Franklin Watts

Franklin Watts Inc.
387 Park Avenue South
New York, NY 10016

Editor: Hazel Poole
Design: K and Co
Consultant: Michael Chinery

Printed in Italy

Library of Congress Cataloging-in-Publication Data

Watts, Barrie.
    Ants / Barrie Watts.
      p. cm. — (Keeping minibeasts)
    Summary: A guide to keeping ants temporarily for the purpose of
observing them.
      ISBN 0-531-14042-3
      1. Ants as pets—Juvenile literature. 2. Ants—Juvenile
literature. [1. Ants as pets. 2. Ants.] I. title. II. Series.
SF459.A47W37   1990
638'.5796—dc20   89-49721
                                                         CIP
                                                          AC

(KEEPING MINIBEASTS)

ANTS

Text and Photographs: Barrie Watts

CONTENTS

Franklin Watts
New York • London • Sydney • Toronto

What are ants?

Ants are very small insects that can be found in almost every country in the world. They are "social" insects, which means that they live together in "colonies."

In a colony there will be at least one queen ant, hundreds of males and thousands of worker ants. Only newly emerged queens and male ants have wings and are able to fly.

Ant colonies make their nests in places where they are protected from the weather and can safely bring up their young. Field ants make earth mound nests in fields and meadows.

Carpenter ants make large nests of small twigs
and leaves around an old tree stump or pole.
Some ants even weave their nests among
leaves high up in tall trees.

Ants are small and fragile so when you collect some, you should be very careful. You will need a plastic box with a tight fitting lid with airholes as ants are good climbers and can easily escape if the lid is not on properly.

Never pick them up with your fingers because you could crush them. You can find ants in spring and summer by looking under rocks or large stones.

Using a small paintbrush, gently brush the ants
— a few at a time — onto a plastic teaspoon.
Carefully put the ants into your container to take
home.

Then place the ants into a small, clear plastic box and keep them out of the sun or else they might die. Use a magnifying glass to study your ants close up.

You can keep ants in a small clear plastic box, such as an aquarium for a few days to observe their behavior. Put earth and stones in the bottom so that it resembles the conditions of their nest site.

Then put a sheet of clear plastic with airholes across the top or the ants will escape. If you are going to keep ants in this way, you will need to provide food such as pieces of fruit, scraps of meat and perhaps a few drops of honey on a flat stone.

Make a formicarium

If you are keeping your ants for a long time, why not make a formicarium for them to live in. This will enable you to see into an ants nest without disturbing them.

You will need some wood, plaster of paris, modeling clay and a sheet of plastic. The clay is used to make a network of tunnels and nesting chambers for the ants on the plastic within a wooden frame.

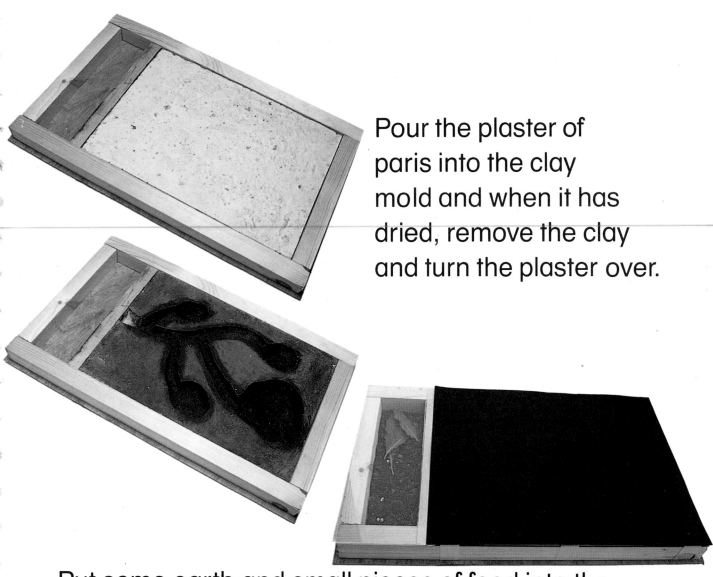

Pour the plaster of paris into the clay mold and when it has dried, remove the clay and turn the plaster over.

Put some earth and small pieces of food into the small feeding area and paint the plaster to make it look natural. When you have finished the formicarium, put it on a window sill out of the sunlight.

Breeding

To keep a colony of ants for breeding, you will need to collect a queen ant and several workers along with some eggs, larvae and pupae (young ants). You will be able to recognize a queen as she will be larger than the other ants. Black garden ants and yellow field ants are fairly common and don't sting!

The ants will need food and you can use honey, small insects and aphids. If the ants like their formicarium and have the right food, they will soon start to multiply.

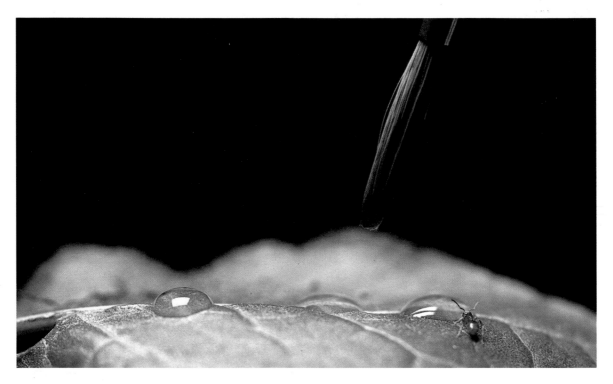

Mix an equal solution of water and honey and put a few drops on a flat stone so that the ants are able to drink it. If you collect a leaf which has aphids on it and put it into the formicarium you will be able to see how the ants milk the aphids to get the sweet honeydew that they feed to their larvae.

Ants also like meat. Put a few scraps into the formicarium and watch them cut it up and take it back to their larvae.

Life-cycle

In an ant colony, only the queen is able to lay eggs. The eggs are tiny, less than 1/10 inch long and are laid in the spring and summer. The worker ants take them from her and put them in "nurseries" where they look after them. They keep them clean and take care of them until they hatch.

The eggs hatch into larvae which are fed by the worker ants. After they have grown to about ¼ inch long, they spin cocoons around themselves. They are then called pupae.

Certain larvae are fed a different and richer food which makes them grow to a bigger size. They will be the new queens.

The pupae are also taken care of by the worker ants. When they are ready to hatch, the workers will help the new adult ants to emerge from their cocoons. They chew at the cocoons so that the ants can struggle out.

New queens have wings when they hatch.
When conditions are suitable, new queen and
male ants will swarm out of the nest and fly
away to mate. The queens will then either go
back to their old nests or form new colonies.

Releasing your ants

When you have finished studying your ants, put them back where you found them. Gently release them so that they can make new nests. Many ants control pests like aphids and caterpillars.

They also make the soil more fertile by adding their discarded food to it. Many ants are our friends, not our enemies.

Queen ants normally only mate once, can live for up to fifteen years and lay thousands and thousands of eggs.

The largest ants are the Bulldog ants from Australia. They can measure up to 3.5 centimeters long.

The army ants of the South American forests have no permanent home. They move from place to place hunting for insects and other creatures in columns of up to 500,000 individuals.

Carpenter ants squirt formic acid from their rear end as a defense against predators. Other ants can sting their attackers just like bees.

Index

TOWNSHIP OF UNION
FREE PUBLIC LIBRARY

J
638.5796
WAT
Watts, Barrie
  Ants.

c.1

8/9/91mw

DEMCO